91157 - 13.95

HUBAND PARK
ELEMENTARY SCHOOL

British Library Cataloguing in Publication Data
Watts, Barrie.
  Stickleback. — (Stopwatch series)
  1. Sticklebacks — Juvenile literature
  I. Title   II. Series
  597'.53   QL638.G27

  ISBN 0-7136-2977-0

Published by A & C Black (Publishers) Limited
35 Bedford Row, London WC1R 4JH

© 1988 Barrie Watts

Acknowledgements
The illustrations are by Helen Senior.
The publishers would like to thank Michael Chinery for his help and advice.

All rights reserved. No part of this publication may be reproduced, stored in a retrieval system, or transmitted in any form or by any means, electronic, mechanical, photocopying, recording or otherwise, without the prior permission of A & C Black (Publishers) Limited.

Filmset by August Filmsetting, Haydock, St. Helens.
Printed in Hong Kong by Dai Nippon Printing Co. Ltd

BLACK CREEK SCHOOL

Stickleback

Barrie Watts

A & C Black · London

Here is a stickleback.

Have you ever seen a stickleback? They live in ponds, lakes, streams and rivers. There are different kinds of stickleback. This one has three spines on its back. It is a bit longer than a matchstick.

Here is a female stickleback.

In winter, the male stickleback is this colour too. But in spring, he changes colour. Look at the big photograph. This is the male in spring.

This book will tell you about the life of a stickleback.

The male stickleback starts to build a nest.

In spring, each male looks for a place to build a nest. When he finds a safe place, he chases other males away.

Here is a male starting to make a nest. First he moves sand and stones to make a small hollow. Can you see the stone in his mouth?

In the big photograph, he is moving his fins very fast to make the water swirl around the hollow. The water pushes more sand out of the hollow.

The male glues some water weeds together.

The male stickleback collects pieces of water weed to put on top of the hollow in the sand.

Look at the big photograph. The male is gluing the weeds together with sticky threads. He makes the threads inside his body.

When he has made a nest of weeds, he wriggles through the middle. This makes a tunnel through the nest.

Eggs grow inside the female stickleback.

While the male stickleback is building his nest, eggs grow inside the female.

When she is ready to lay her eggs, the female waits near the surface of the water. She swims with her head slightly upwards, like this.

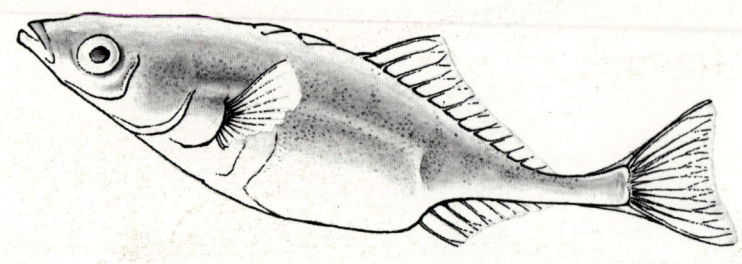

Look at the big photograph. The female stickleback has a fat stomach because she has lots of eggs inside her. She can carry as many as a hundred eggs in her body.

The female follows the male to his nest.

When the male spots a fat female, he swims towards her. He does a zigzag dance. This is called a courtship dance.

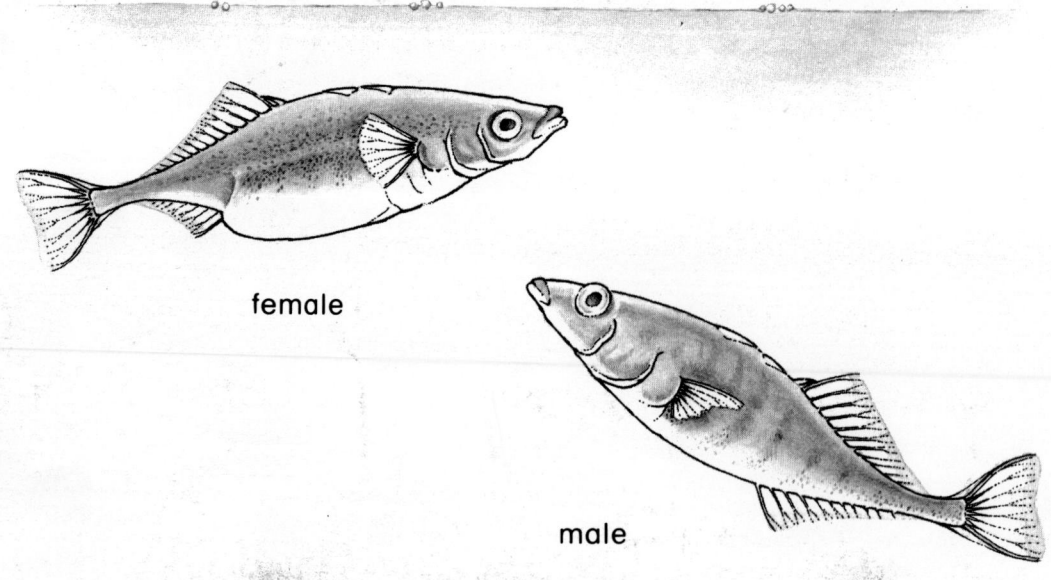

female

male

Then the male swims towards his nest. If the female is ready to lay her eggs, she follows him. The male lies on his side and points to the entrance with his nose.

In the big photograph, the female is wriggling into the tunnel in the middle of the nest.

The female lays her eggs in the nest.

Look at the photograph. Can you see the female's tail sticking out of the nest? She is laying her eggs in the nest. To make the female lay her eggs, the male touches her tail.

After the female has laid her eggs, she leaves the nest. The male then swims through the nest and covers the eggs with a milky liquid from his body.

The eggs can now develop into baby sticklebacks.

The male chases the female away from the nest. Later, he may try to make more females lay eggs in his nest.

The male stickleback looks after the eggs.

To hide the nest from enemies, the male picks up sand in his mouth and spits it on top of the nest.

Look at the photograph. The male stickleback is waving his fins to and fro to push plenty of clean, fresh water over the eggs. This helps the baby sticklebacks to develop properly.

The male stickleback guards the nest.

The male protects the nest from enemies which might eat the eggs. Here he is chasing off another male stickleback.

In the photograph, the male is attacking a large snail.
He will hit the snail with his open mouth until it crawls away.
Can you see that his spines are standing up? This makes him look more dangerous.

The baby sticklebacks grow inside the eggs.

After seven days, the eggs look like this.

Can you see the two black dots inside each egg?
These are the eyes of the baby sticklebacks.

In the big photograph, you can see the eyes more clearly.
Inside each egg, a baby fish is curled into a ball.
These three eggs are shown very large. In real life,
each one is only as big as the top of a pin.

Tiny sticklebacks come out of the eggs.

After ten days, the baby sticklebacks break out of the eggs. They cannot swim properly yet.

The male watches over his family. Here he is picking up a young fish in his mouth to take it back to the nest.

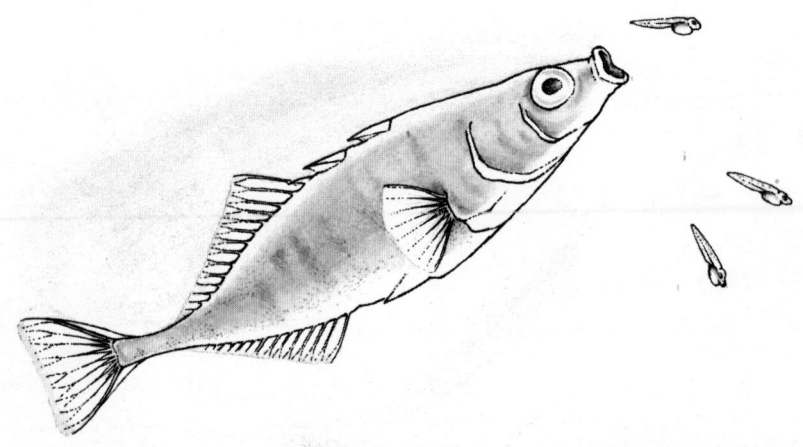

A young stickleback gets its food from a ball of yolk, which is joined to its stomach. Can you see the ball of yolk in the photograph?

Inside the ball of yolk is a small drop of oil. This helps the young fish to float because oil is lighter than water.

The young sticklebacks grow bigger.

Twelve days after they come out of the eggs, the sticklebacks are about as long as your fingernail. They can swim well and find water fleas and tiny worms to eat.

The stickleback in the big photograph is three months old. It is nearly as long as a matchstick. By next spring, it will be as big as its parents. If it is a male, it will change colour and build a nest.

What do you think will happen then?

BLACK CREEK SCHOOL

Stickleback

Barrie Watts

A & C Black · London

Here is a stickleback.

Have you ever seen a stickleback? They live in ponds, lakes, streams and rivers. There are different kinds of stickleback. This one has three spines on its back. It is a bit longer than a matchstick.

Here is a female stickleback.

In winter, the male stickleback is this colour too. But in spring, he changes colour. Look at the big photograph. This is the male in spring.

This book will tell you about the life of a stickleback.

2

The male stickleback starts to build a nest.

In spring, each male looks for a place to build a nest. When he finds a safe place, he chases other males away.

Here is a male starting to make a nest. First he moves sand and stones to make a small hollow. Can you see the stone in his mouth?

In the big photograph, he is moving his fins very fast to make the water swirl around the hollow. The water pushes more sand out of the hollow.

The male glues some water weeds together.

The male stickleback collects pieces of water weed to put on top of the hollow in the sand.

Look at the big photograph. The male is gluing the weeds together with sticky threads. He makes the threads inside his body.

When he has made a nest of weeds, he wriggles through the middle. This makes a tunnel through the nest.

Eggs grow inside the female stickleback.

While the male stickleback is building his nest, eggs grow inside the female.

When she is ready to lay her eggs, the female waits near the surface of the water. She swims with her head slightly upwards, like this.

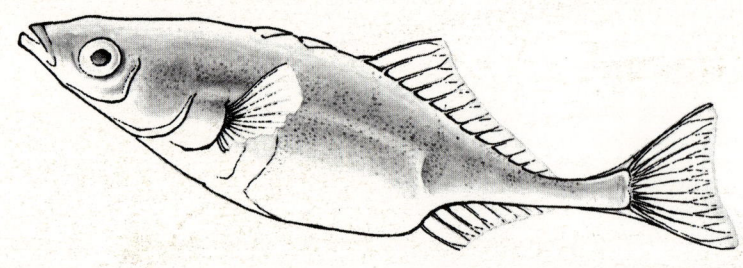

Look at the big photograph. The female stickleback has a fat stomach because she has lots of eggs inside her. She can carry as many as a hundred eggs in her body.

The female follows the male to his nest.

When the male spots a fat female, he swims towards her. He does a zigzag dance. This is called a courtship dance.

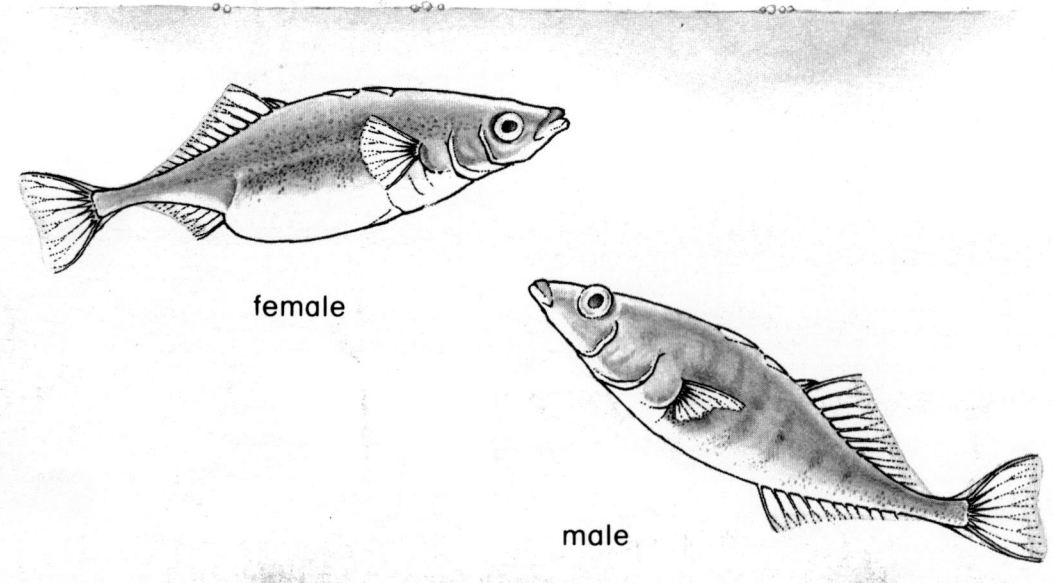

female

male

Then the male swims towards his nest. If the female is ready to lay her eggs, she follows him. The male lies on his side and points to the entrance with his nose.

In the big photograph, the female is wriggling into the tunnel in the middle of the nest.

The female lays her eggs in the nest.

Look at the photograph. Can you see the female's tail sticking out of the nest? She is laying her eggs in the nest. To make the female lay her eggs, the male touches her tail.

After the female has laid her eggs, she leaves the nest. The male then swims through the nest and covers the eggs with a milky liquid from his body.

The eggs can now develop into baby sticklebacks.

The male chases the female away from the nest. Later, he may try to make more females lay eggs in his nest.

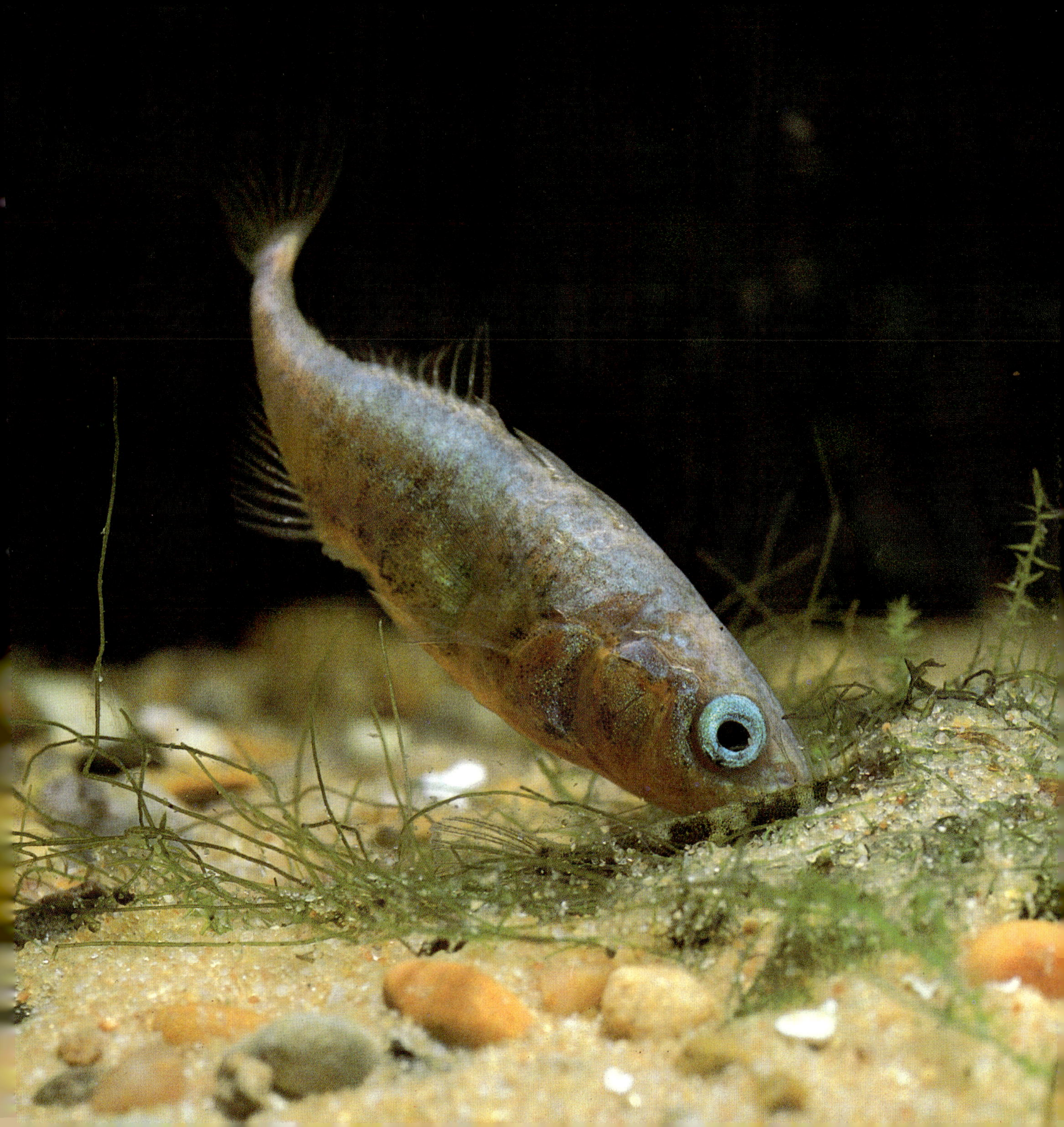

The male stickleback looks after the eggs.

To hide the nest from enemies, the male picks up sand in his mouth and spits it on top of the nest.

Look at the photograph. The male stickleback is waving his fins to and fro to push plenty of clean, fresh water over the eggs. This helps the baby sticklebacks to develop properly.

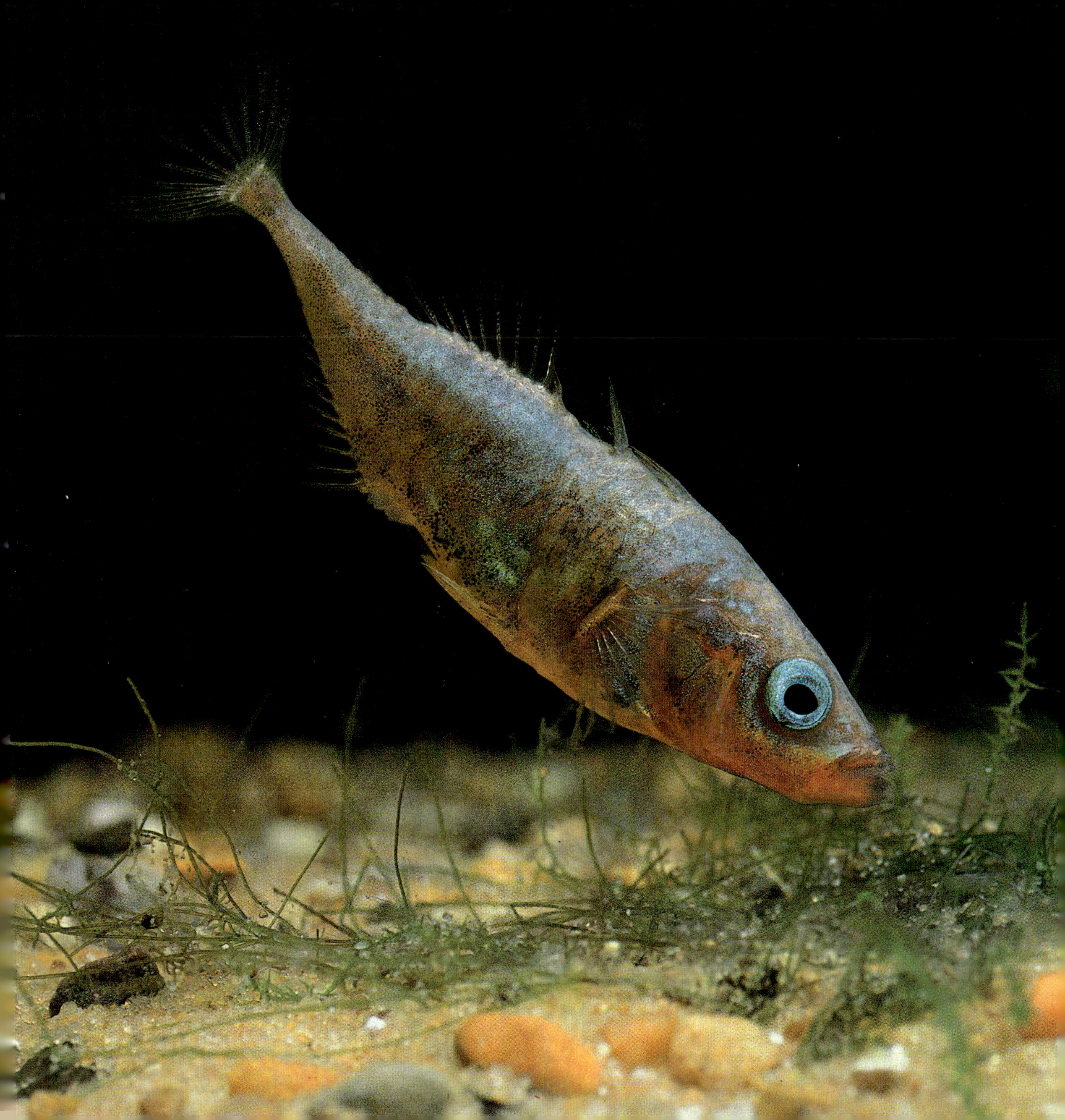

The male stickleback guards the nest.

The male protects the nest from enemies which might eat the eggs. Here he is chasing off another male stickleback.

In the photograph, the male is attacking a large snail. He will hit the snail with his open mouth until it crawls away. Can you see that his spines are standing up? This makes him look more dangerous.

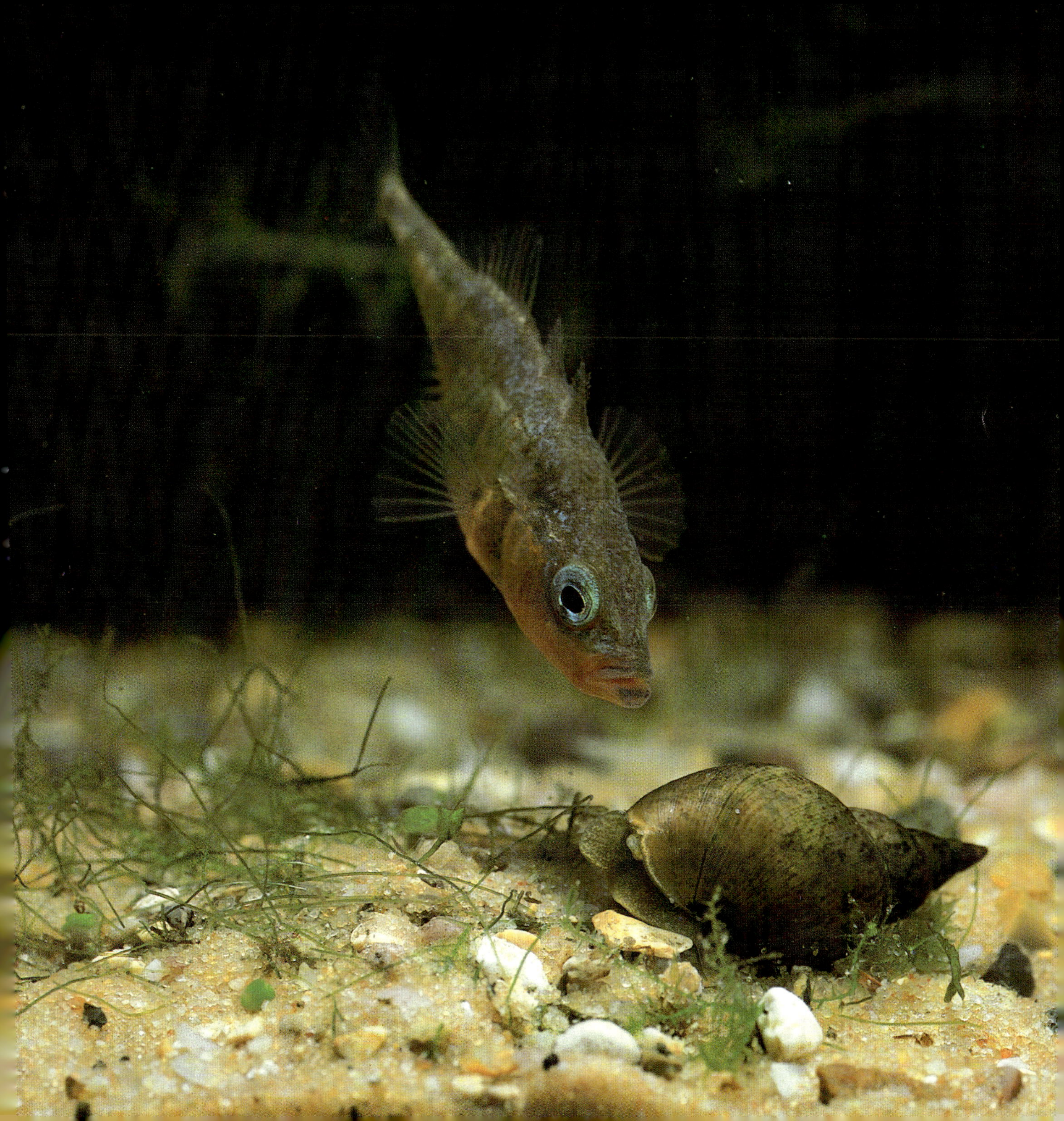

The baby sticklebacks grow inside the eggs.

After seven days, the eggs look like this.

Can you see the two black dots inside each egg?
These are the eyes of the baby sticklebacks.

In the big photograph, you can see the eyes more clearly.
Inside each egg, a baby fish is curled into a ball.
These three eggs are shown very large. In real life,
each one is only as big as the top of a pin.

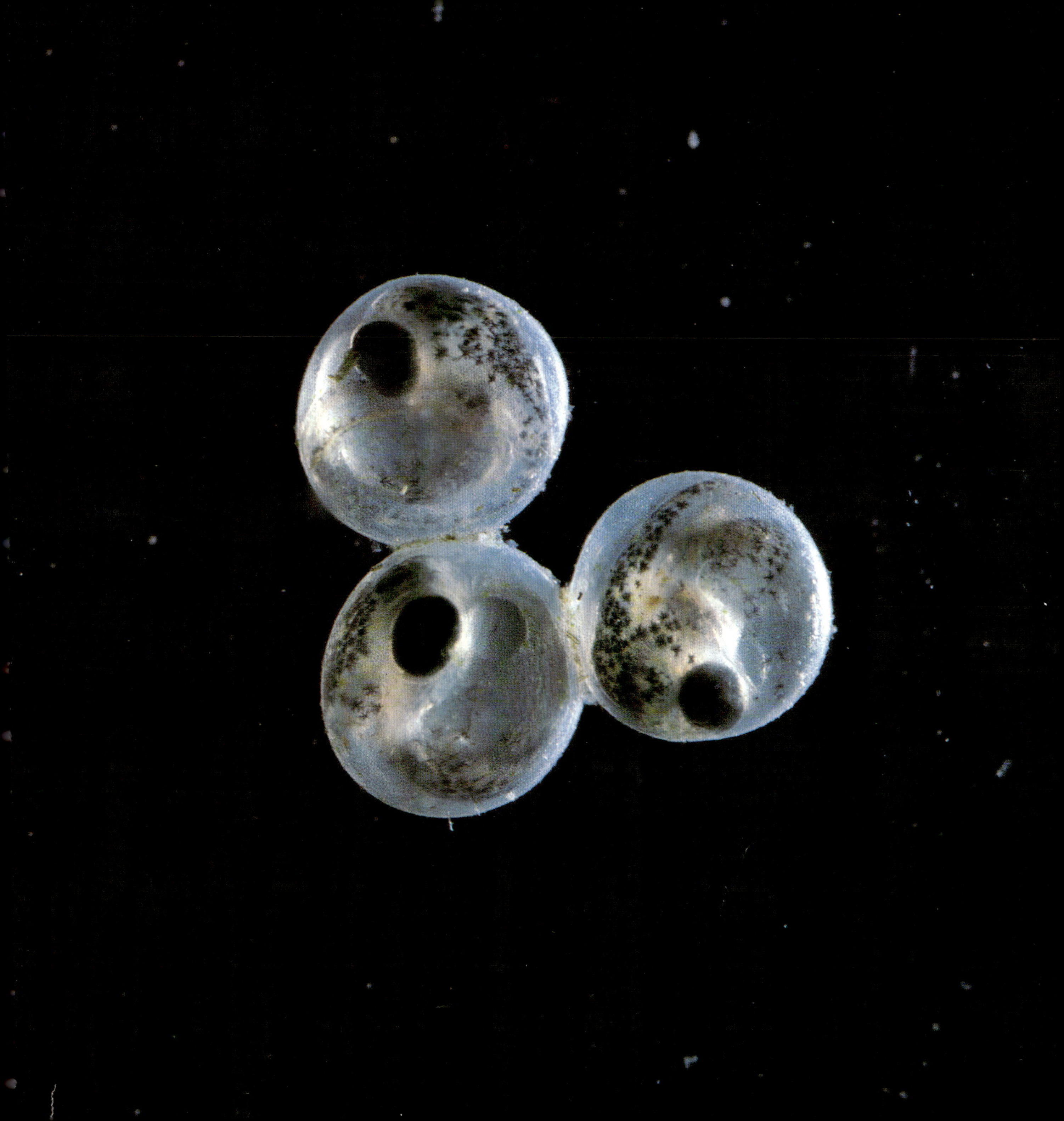

Tiny sticklebacks come out of the eggs.

After ten days, the baby sticklebacks break out of the eggs. They cannot swim properly yet.

The male watches over his family. Here he is picking up a young fish in his mouth to take it back to the nest.

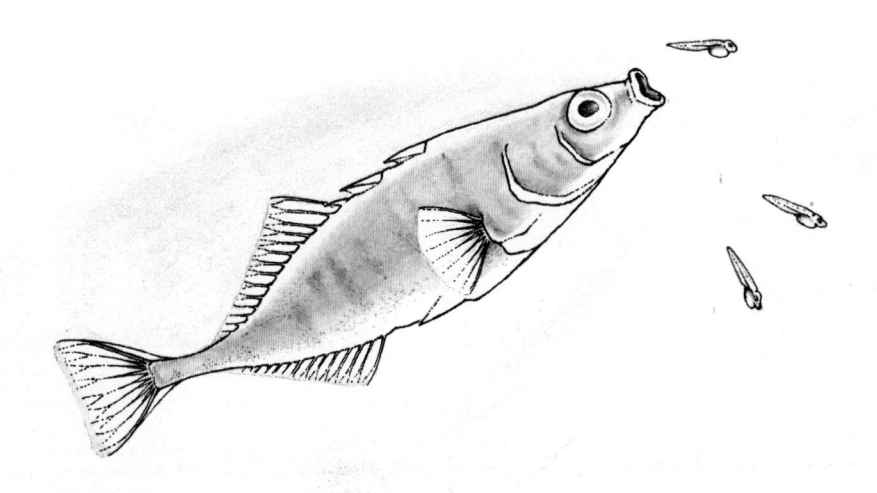

A young stickleback gets its food from a ball of yolk, which is joined to its stomach. Can you see the ball of yolk in the photograph?

Inside the ball of yolk is a small drop of oil. This helps the young fish to float because oil is lighter than water.

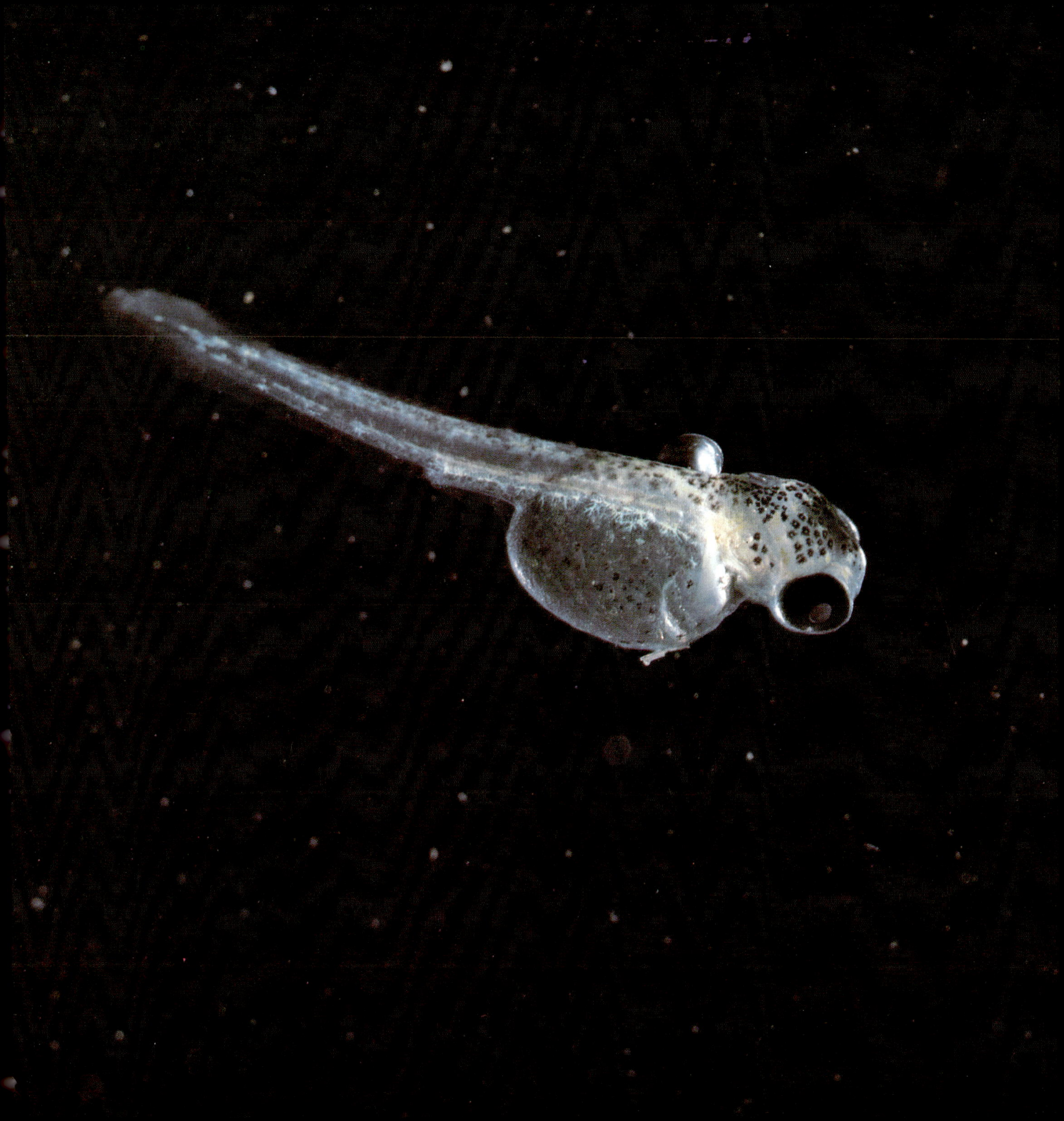

The young sticklebacks grow bigger.

Twelve days after they come out of the eggs, the sticklebacks are about as long as your fingernail. They can swim well and find water fleas and tiny worms to eat.

The stickleback in the big photograph is three months old. It is nearly as long as a matchstick. By next spring, it will be as big as its parents. If it is a male, it will change colour and build a nest.

What do you think will happen then?

Do you remember how a stickleback looks after its young?
See if you can tell the story in your own words.
You can use these pictures to help you.

1

2

4

5

Index

This index will help you to find some of the important words in the book.

babies 12, 14, 18, 20

courtship dance 10

eggs 8, 10, 12, 14, 16, 18, 20
enemies 16
eyes 18

female 2, 8, 10, 12
fins 4, 14
food 20, 22

gluing 6

male 2, 4, 6, 10, 12, 14, 16, 20

nest 4, 6, 10, 12, 14

spines 2, 16
spring 2, 4
sticky threads 6
swim 8, 10, 12, 20, 22

tail 12

water weed 6

yolk 20

Look out for sticklebacks in ponds and streams.
In spring, see if you can find a male looking after his nest.
Make sure you don't disturb the fishes and don't take them home.